JAPANESE SPIDER CRABS

Emma Bassier

DiscoverRoo
An Imprint of Pop!
popbooksonline.com

abdobooks.com

Published by Pop!, a division of ABDO, PO Box 398166,
Minneapolis, Minnesota 55439. Copyright © 2020 by POP,
LLC. International copyrights reserved in all countries. No
part of this book may be reproduced in any form without
written permission from the publisher. Pop!™ is a trademark
and logo of POP, LLC.

Printed in the United States of America, North Mankato,
Minnesota.

102019
012020   THIS BOOK CONTAINS
         RECYCLED MATERIALS

Cover Photo: Shutterstock Images
Interior Photos: Shutterstock Images, 1, 6, 7, 11, 12–13, 17
(top), 19, 20–21, 22, 25, 26, 27, 28, 31; iStockphoto, 5, 12,
16 (top), 23, 29, 30; Imaginechina/AP Images, 8; Red Line
Editorial, 9; Dave Thompson/PA Wire URN:16075615/Press
Association/AP Images, 14–15; Mauro Rodrigues/Alamy, 16–17

Editor: Nick Rebman
Series Designer: Jake Slavik

Library of Congress Control Number: 2019942479
Publisher's Cataloging-in-Publication Data

Names: Bassier, Emma, author.

Title: Japanese spider crabs / by Emma Bassier

Description: Minneapolis, Minnesota : Pop!, 2020 | Series:
    Weird and wonderful animals | Includes online resources
    and index.

Identifiers: ISBN 9781532166051 (lib. bdg.) | ISBN
    9781644943359 (pbk.) | ISBN 9781532167379 (ebook)

Subjects: LCSH: Spider crabs--Juvenile literature. | Crabs--
    Behavior--Juvenile literature. | Oddities--Juvenile
    literature. | Crustaceans--Juvenile literature. | Marine
    animals--Juvenile literature.

Classification: DDC 595.3842--dc23

WELCOME TO
DiscoverRoo!

Pop open this book and you'll find QR codes loaded

with information, so you can learn even more!

Scan this code* and others

like it while you read, or visit

the website below to make

this book pop!

popbooksonline.com/japanese-spider-crabs

*Scanning QR codes requires a web-enabled smart device with a QR code reader app and a camera.

TABLE OF CONTENTS

CHAPTER 1
THE WORLD'S LARGEST CRAB

Deep in the ocean, a massive crab crawls across the seafloor. Its long legs move slowly over the sand. The Japanese spider crab is the largest crab in the world. Its enormous legs can span up to 15 feet (4.6 m).

WATCH A VIDEO HERE!

Japanese spider crabs do not move quickly.

Lobsters have much shorter legs than Japanese spider crabs.

The Japanese spider crab is an

arthropod. This group of animals

includes spiders, insects, lobsters, and

other crabs. These animals do not have skin. Instead, every arthropod has a hard outer layer called an **exoskeleton**.

DID YOU KNOW?

The Japanese name for this crab is *taka-ashi-gani*, which means "tall legs crab."

An exoskeleton protects the soft parts inside the crab's body.

Scientists use underwater vehicles called submersibles to explore the deep sea.

The Japanese spider crab lives in the Pacific Ocean near Japan. It lives up to 2,000 feet (600 m) below the surface. The water there is dark and cold. This deep **habitat** makes the crab hard for scientists to study.

RANGE MAP

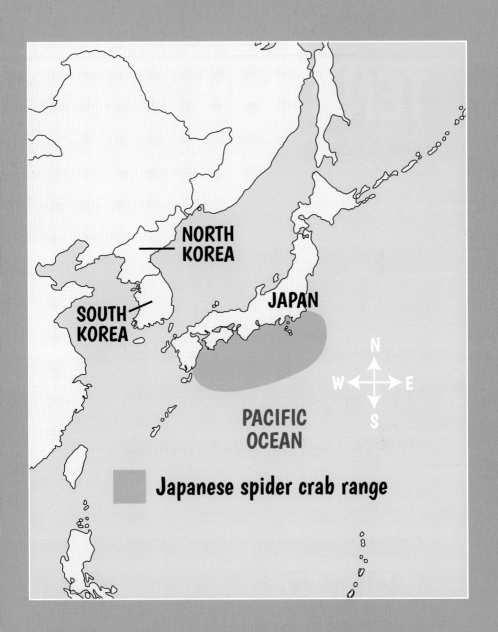

NORTH KOREA

SOUTH KOREA

JAPAN

N
W   E
S

PACIFIC OCEAN

Japanese spider crab range

CHAPTER 2
TEN LONG LEGS

The Japanese spider crab has ten long legs. Eight of the crab's legs have pointed tips. The tips hook into cracks in rocks. These legs help the crab climb. The other two legs are called **chelipeds**. These legs have sharp claws at the end.

LEARN MORE HERE!

cheliped

On male Japanese spider crabs, the chelipeds are longer than the other legs.

The Japanese spider crab is orange

with white spots. Short, stubby eyes

stick out from the front of its body.

The bottom of the crab's body is mostly flat. On its back, the crab has a thick shell called a carapace.

A Japanese spider crab can weigh up to 44 pounds (20 kg).

Short, spiky bumps cover the shell.

When a crab becomes too big for its

shell, the crab **molts**. It gets rid of its

old shell and forms a new one.

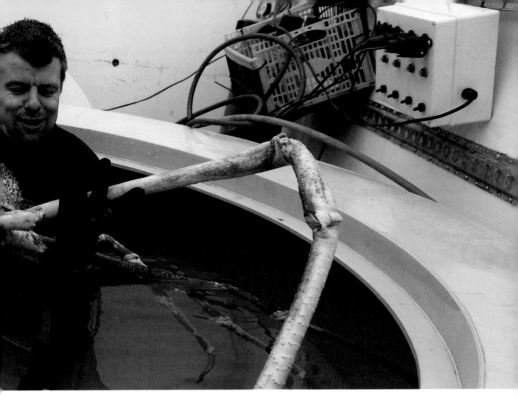

A scientist helps a Japanese spider crab move into a new tank at an aquarium.

DID YOU KNOW?

A Japanese spider crab can decorate its shell with pieces of plants. Then its bumpy shell blends in with rocks.

LIFE CYCLE OF A JAPANESE SPIDER CRAB

The eggs hatch into larvae. Larvae are animals early in their life cycle.

Females lay up to 1.5 million eggs each year. Only a few eggs survive.

Japanese spider crabs can live up to 100 years.

The larvae molt as they grow.

Larvae molt multiple times in their first year. After four molts, they are small crabs.

Young crabs grow over time. They molt less often as they get bigger.

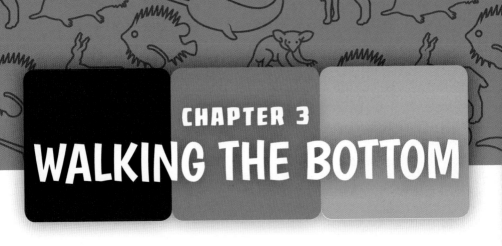

CHAPTER 3
WALKING THE BOTTOM

Japanese spider crabs cannot swim.

Instead, they walk along the seafloor.

They find shelter in holes. The crabs are

not aggressive. They rarely hunt. Most of

the time, they **scavenge** for food. They

eat whatever they can find.

COMPLETE AN ACTIVITY HERE!

A Japanese spider crab takes shelter near a rock.

Japanese spider crabs spend most of their time looking for food.

Japanese spider crabs may eat dead animals that sink down to the ocean floor. Sometimes they eat parts of plants. They scrape the plants off rocks. The crabs use their claws to grab food. For example, they hold shelled animals such as mollusks. Next, they break open the hard shells. Then, they pinch the flesh out.

Octopuses are one of the few predators that Japanese spider crabs face.

Japanese spider crabs do not have

many **predators**. Octopuses and other

types of crabs may try to eat them. But

most animals stay out of their way.

DID YOU KNOW?

Some animals, such as sponges and anemones, can grow on the shells of Japanese spider crabs.

Sponges are underwater animals that come in a wide variety of colors.

CHAPTER 4
GROWING BIGGER AND OLDER

Japanese spider crabs grow in bursts.

Crabs **molt** more often when they

are young. During this time, they grow

quickly. But when they reach their adult

size, they molt less often.

LEARN MORE HERE!

Young spider crabs tend to live in shallow waters, but adults live in deeper waters.

DID YOU KNOW?

Scientists think Japanese spider crabs can survive with up to three missing legs.

A Japanese spider crab's legs grow longer as the animal ages.

Each new shell takes time to harden.

As a result, the crab is in danger during

this time. **Predators** have an easier time attacking the crab when its shell is soft.

When necessary, Japanese spider crabs may use their claws to protect themselves.

MISSING LEGS

Many Japanese spider crabs lose legs during attacks. But crabs can survive with missing legs. They can also grow new legs when they molt. However, molting takes lots of energy. Some crabs, especially old ones, may die after they molt.

Female spider crabs can lay more than one million eggs every year. Very few of the eggs grow into adults.

Japanese spider crabs can live up to 100 years. They live alone most of the time. But once a year, they **migrate** to mate. They mate in shallow waters that are only 160 feet (50 m) deep.

A law in Japan protects the crabs. Fishing boats cannot catch them during mating season. This law helps keep the crab population stable.

In Japan, seafood markets sell many kinds of crabs.

MAKING CONNECTIONS

TEXT-TO-SELF

Have you ever seen an animal with an exoskeleton? What kind of animal was it?

TEXT-TO-TEXT

Have you read books about other animals that live on the ocean floor? How do those animals find food?

TEXT-TO-WORLD

Scientists still haven't learned everything about Japanese spider crabs. Why do you think the crab's habitat makes it hard to study?

GLOSSARY

cheliped – a leg with a claw at the end.

exoskeleton – a hard outer layer that covers an animal's body.

habitat – the area where an animal normally lives.

migrate – to move from one area to another at a certain time.

molt – to get rid of an old covering and form a new one.

predator – an animal that hunts other animals for food.

scavenge – to eat anything that is available, often animals that are already dead.

INDEX

ONLINE RESOURCES

popbooksonline.com

Scan this code* and others like it while you read, or visit the website below to make this book pop!

popbooksonline.com/japanese-spider-crabs

*Scanning QR codes requires a web-enabled smart device with a QR code reader app and a camera.